THE
LEADING MAN

by Stephen J. Blakesley

Forward

The Leading Man

Barbara Kellerman, once the James MacGregor Burns lecturer in public leadership at the Harvard Kennedy School, in her book *The End of Leadership*, (published as late as 2012) wrote that there were some *1500 definitions* of **Leadership** and *40 theories* of such. It is now 2018, and there are likely an even a greater number of definitions and theories. It is my objective, in this book, not to propose another definition or present an additional theory but to condense and simplify those processes and definitions of leading, so that we can all understand and pursue the course that best fits and meets our needs and wishes.

I have always believed that it is not possible to become or achieve a goal that is not understood or clearly defined, except by pure luck. Thus, to begin, I propose that we accept this definition of leadership: *The process of influencing followers to join in the pursuit of a commonly held objective.*

Yes, I do believe that there are other acceptable definitions, but this one is brief and simple. If achieved, however, it frequently produces the desired result, i.e., **the accomplishment of the goal.**

To be clear, let's first look at some of the words in this definition.

First, we call it a "process," and a logical question is what exactly is a process? In this case, *a process is a series of actions or steps, that, if taken, will likely achieve a result.*

Second, leading depends greatly upon one's ability to "influence" others, and our ability to do that is determined by the presence we emit and our capacity to communicate a vision (end goal).

Third, is the introduction of a group known as followers. Just what or who are followers? Well, a *follower,* in this instance, is a subordinate, with less power, authority, and influence than his or her superior (the leader or leaders). Thus, in many ways, a leader's task is that of motivating others to aid or join them in the pursuit of a proposed goal or objective. So, to be a leader, you must have, at least one follower (someone who believes in the goal) and be able to motivate him or her to move in the direction desired.

What, then, are the essential attributes of a LEADER?   **That is the question!**

Chapter I

What's to Come?

with Clarity

Specifically, if you want to become an exceptional leader, here are six BASIC and ESSENTIAL skills all leaders must have:

1. **Presence**
2. **Visioning**
3. **Communication**
4. **Motivation**
5. **Crediting**
6. **Emotional Intelligence**

Some insight into the meaning of each:

Presence: *The image one presents*

Visioning: *The future one sees*

Communicating: *The words one speaks and hears*

Motivating: *The reason one acts*

Crediting: *The humility one displays*

Emotional Intelligence: *The emotion you feel and apply*

Presence. It is true that people should not judge you, at least, initially. But, the fact is, they do. It is just going to happen, so get out in front and give them a memorable image that will capture their attention both now and in the future.

Visioning is one's ability to see the future. People want specificity in their future, and most want to be part of something bigger than themselves. A compelling vision is often inspirational, then motivating.

Communicating has a specific importance and value. One can have the most compelling vision in the world, but if you can't communicate it and get "buy-in" from others, it will have little, if any, impact.

Motivating. A leader's job is to gather followers and direct their efforts toward the goal. Thus, the first three leadership attributes (presence, visioning, and communicating) must be developed beyond what one might term "average." One must have a special presence to get people to listen; then, the vision they present must be exciting enough to capture their imagination; and, finally, the leader must have a unique ability to communicate the vision in such a way that the team pursues it, with passion.

Crediting. Giving credit to others for work done is a big part of humility and leadership. Giving credit to those deserving it is a skill many do not have but still must learn. Helping others to feel good about themselves is a valued skill.

Emotional Intelligence. The final attribute, yet possibly the most important attribute necessary for good leadership, is a skill and can be learned. It's place among the important factors or attributes of leadership, though presented last, may be the MOST important of all the six basic leadership attributes. We believe you cannot sustain a leadership role without *emotional intelligence*. So, take the time and spend the money to establish your emotional skills.

There are only six basic leadership attributes mentioned here. All are important. Competency in all six is the beginning of exceptional leadership. Leverage your existing attributes wherever possible but commit to "advancing the envelope" (getting better everyday). Improving a little in each and every day is the objective. Just remember: Before you start working to improve others, make certain you are "the best **you** can be."

When you reach that point, you will have arrived at a place where you can, effectively, help others.

Chapter II

Presence

People Shouldn't Judge

Maybe that's right, people shouldn't judge; unfortunately, they do. Yes, maybe some don't, but most do. So, first impressions are important. They are important because first impressions are likely the determinant of whether you are heard. Making a good first impression is an effort of efficiency. If you make a good first impression, you will be heard before others who fail in this respect.

Realizing that it is difficult to overcome a bad first impression, let's get ahead of the game and dive into the meaning of this mystical word **Presence**. What is "presence" and how do you get it or create it?

In her book *Executive Presence*, Sylvia Ann Hewlett summarized nearly two years of research on the topic of presence by suggesting that "executive presence" consists of only three things:

- How you act (gravitas)
- How you speak (communication)
- How you look (appearance)

She suggested that these three attributes (gravitas, communication, and appearance) were universal; moreover, establishing a presence is an essential task for an aspiring leader. Capturing the attention of others is job number one.

If others don't notice you or you are not able to get their attention by simply being there, you will likely have difficulty getting them to listen to anything you might have to say. People who have a presence get the attention of others.

My mother used to tell me, "Stevie" (she really didn't call me "Stevie," it just makes a better story). Anyway, she said to me, "Stevie, if you keep your mouth shut, people won't know how dumb you are."

I did not like it much at the time, but, after thinking about it, I concluded that she was right, *what you don't say never hurts you and at times may help*. But, while it might be important to be the "silent type," one could say that when you do speak, the content needs to be accurate, believable, and inspirational. Thus, at an early age, I learned to speak without speaking. I learned how to make my presence known. So, what can we do to improve our presence, apart from being accurate, believable, and significant? How can we improve?

Improving presence begins with adding to our *gravitas*. "Gravitas" is an interesting word that few of us can clearly define. One of the best definitions I have heard in a long time comes from Sylvia Hewlett, as mentioned earlier. She suggests that gravitas has six parts, i.e., confidence, decisiveness, integrity, emotional intelligence, reputation, and charisma.

The improvement of any of those is easier said than done. Improving gravitas seems to be about what we perceive or what someone exudes. Controlling what we exude is a challenge. Our perception of others is important. Do they display a confidence? Is there a decisiveness about them? Do they do what they say? Do they understand how the event has an impact on others? Do their deeds precede them? Do they exude charisma? Are their goals clear? Are they dedicated to the achievement of their goals? All of these make up gravitas and have an impact on presence. Gravitas is, by far, the weightiest (67%) of the three factors contributing to one's presence.

The second most important factor in the creation of presence is *communication* (28%). Is this person a skilled communicator? What is it that identifies someone as a skilled communicator? Just understanding what it is that makes one a good communicator is important. There are just three prevalent ways one communicates, i.e., by words, by body language, and by the inflection one gives to those words.

Words. The size of your vocabulary sends a message of who you are. Many different research projects lend credibility to the thought that the greater your vocabulary, the more successful you will be. Of course, there are exceptions to everything, but to improve your vocabulary, the size of it sends a positive message of who you are.

Inflection. Would you rather listen to Roseanne Barr or James Earl Jones? Speaking in an optimally appealing tone (125 Hz) was found to be important. The higher the pitch of your voice, the less you are heard. For instance, James Earl Jones speaks at about 85 Hz and Roseanne Barr at about 377 Hz. There has been much study of the pitch of one's voice and one's ability to earn big money. A 22 Hz drop in voice frequency correlates to an increase of $187,000 increase in annual earnings. The lesson here is that the lower the voice, the more the presence is enhanced.

And, finally, but most importantly, it is **body language** that says more than anything else. It is showing signs that you care and are paying attention that makes a big dent in your being heard. A good example is how distracting the cell-phone really is and how detrimental it can be to one's image. Paying attention to your cell-phone when other things are happening is certainly a "no-no." It is so disrespectful for someone to be texting or reading a message while someone else is talking or presenting. Another distraction is the carrying on of side conversations while others are talking. Just knowing how to show respect contributes greatly to one's presence.

So, to add value to your communication skills and increase your presence, you might consider reading *How to Win Friends and Influence People* by Dale Carnegie or *Ask More* by Frank Sesno. Maybe you may want to analyze your voice and make the necessary adjustment or pay less attention to your cell-phone.

The third and final aspect of presence is *appearance* (5%). There are just two important points here, and one has to do with your physical appearance. Here's an example of what I mean: Once I was on a plane to some destination, and the gentleman across the aisle from me was amazingly distracting. The hairs in his ears had grown to such a state that they appeared like one of those Chia pets where grass grew in all directions on either side of his head. The hair in his ears or, I should say, out of his ears was such that I was amazed as to how he could even hear. I would not follow that guy.

Another example is bad teeth. They can, sometimes, be more distracting than what a person is saying. So, paying attention to how you look is a key piece to creating the presence you wish to exude.

One of the most valuable things my mother gave to me was a sense of color-matching. She was a real teacher when it came to the certainty, i.e., clothes colors matched and what clothes to wear for which occasion. Admittedly, appearance is only 5% of presence, but sometimes little things mean a lot. Cut the hair in your ears and nose, fix your teeth if needed, and make certain your clothes reflect the image you wish to present.

It is important to understand that **presence** does not come with the title but rather as a precursor of leadership. It is true that some think that one becomes a leader first and then develops presence, but it is the other way around, i.e., exhibit the presence, and you will get the hearing and attention you deserve.

Nothing will cause a "short circuit" in your leadership efforts quicker than poor appearance.

Chapter III

Visioning

Where Are We Going?

Leaders are going places. I believe we would all agree that it would be difficult to be a leader without a compelling, future destination, i.e., a **Vision**.

There is a story behind the singer Willie Nelson being asked: What is a leader? His response was: *Someone who walks fast and gets out in front of a group of people marching in the same direction.* I wish it was so simple. If you are looking for a novel definition of leadership that one might be it, but, realistically, a leader is a lot more than someone walking fast.

Leaders are those, at least in part, who can visualize a desirable destination or several destinations that others can get excited about.

Being a visionary doesn't make you a leader, but you will not likely be a leader without being a **visionary**. Here are some foundation attributes of visionaries I have known:

- They know who they are (self-awareness)
- They know their values and purpose
- They know where they want to go
- They realize the value of "buy-in"
- They have a positive attitude
- They advance the envelope every day

Some key thoughts leaders are constantly considering are:

First, the most important thing you need to know is the place from where you are starting. You must know, with certainty, from where you are beginning. And the more accurate you are on this one, the easier it is to craft a plan to reach some exciting place in the future.

Second, the most important piece of information is what your values are and what your purpose is.

Third is knowing where you want to go.

Fourth is the ability required of leaders to get others to buy-in.

Fifth is the ability to find the "silver lining" in all you do. Remember that there will always be obstacles.

Sixth is realizing that you can't usually get to where you want to go, instantaneously, but you can make positive progress every day (advance the envelope every day).

We do believe the reason many visions are not achieved is because they are too complicated. Even though "simplifying" is not one of the core essentials of leadership, it may be one of those nonessentials but necessaries. One main task for a leader is to make certain the people he/she works with understands the vision.

Understanding may require the leader to "break it down" so that others can comprehend "what's in it for them."

A vision is an essential part of moving forward, so the more clarity the better. If one understands where one is and where one is going, then the plan to most effectively get to the destination is another critical task needing to be completed. Thought and preparation must go into the making of the plan, but the plan needs to be flexible, as sometimes obstacles occur that were not anticipated. Milestones need be set to monitor progress.

Just to exemplify how important occasional checking of progress is, think of this example: *If one is here on Earth and going to the Moon, a specific trajectory is important and, if nothing changes, will lead us to our destination: the Moon. However, we all know that things do change, and, if we are only one degree off, just one degree, we could miss the destination, totally.* So, checking the progress with the destination and adjusting is a critical part to the accomplishment of the vision.

Chapter IV

Communication

What's in It for Me?

Communication is, certainly, one of the most important attributes of a leader. For instance, you can have great visions, but if you can't communicate them, you and the vision are of little or no value. You can resolve great conflicts, for instance, but only through skillful communication. You can motivate others, but communication lies at the heart of being able to move others. The list goes on and on.

Communication has two parts, i.e., speaking and listening. Both are important, but there is far more written on "speaking" than "listening." So, let's hit the easiest first. Speaking has three parts: words, inflection, and body language. For the most part, we have covered the "body language" piece in a previous chapter, so I want to take a quick look at the "words" part, primarily.

First, let's consider the environment from which you frequently speak. It usually comes with one uncertainty. If you are a leader (or hope to be one), while you are sharing the direction you want your group to go, the group is thinking "what's in it for us?" They are saying or at least thinking: "That might be good for him, but what do we get out of it?" If you are going to be a successful leader, you must be skillful at answering that question.

So, the next big step, in becoming a good leader, is learning to use powerful, persuasive, and passionate words.

Becoming a good communicator requires more than increasing your vocabulary, however. There are studies that suggest that individuals with a larger vocabulary make better leaders. But that is far "in the weeds." Let's talk about that another day.

To continue our discussion on **Communication**, let's begin with some research. Sixteen thousand words are spoken daily by the average individual, and not all those words are positive ones. We have all had the experience of saying something that, well let's just say, was less than positive, something we would have said in a different way, if we had the opportunity to say it again. It is not likely that we will eliminate every occasion in which we offend someone else or speak things that were somewhat less than factual, but we can get better at it. Speaking of being heard, there are just a few basics I want to cover with you.

It is generally accepted and proven, by varied research projects, that people like and thus listen more to people who are like themselves. So, it may be worthwhile to know the general culture of those, to whom, you are speaking. Maybe the first effort is one of finding those like one's self to cement the vision and get them to be among the first followers. There is much research that shows people will follow the first followers rather than the leader who influenced the follower.

Coming up with great ideas is easy; selling them to others is much harder. That legendary image maker Ron Popeil of Ronco fame was a master communicator. Remember that guy? He not only looked perfect, he made everything he sold look the same: Perfect. He realized that people want change and are constantly on the lookout for it. He guided them through memories and present events. He made everything perfect, so perfect we felt as if we could not do without whatever it was he was selling. Now that is communication on multiple levels. All of which required great and accurate knowledge of those watching and how they were feeling.

Chapter V

Motivation

Why?

Motivation is the why you do things and why others do them as well. As a leader and as part of improving your leadership skills, I encourage you to know yourself, i.e., to become *self-aware*. Time spent understanding yourself is never wasted. But there is yet another piece that is equally important: *Knowing others*.

A leader is charged with both knowing the self and knowing others. Knowing the "why" of his/her life and the lives of others is a demanding but beneficial task. Why people do the things they do, both good and bad, is the beginning of a leader's edge. It is one of those things that make a leader good or bad.

An older but frequently effective means of motivation is what we know as the carrot and stick method, i.e., old reward and punishment method. What research has found, and experience has proven, is that the carrot and stick method works some of the time. It does seem to be more effective where both we and others are focused on a task type of objective. Daniel Pink, in his book *Drive*, points to some of the flaws of the carrot and stick method of motivation.

1. It can suppress internal motivation
2. Performance can be diminished
3. Creativity can be oppressed
4. Good behavior can be suppressed
5. It can encourage unethical behavior

In most cases, none of these outcomes is a good one. So, in both self-motivation and motivation of others, being able to answer the question *why* is almost essential to finding the key.

Some years back, the Gallop organization surveyed the workforce and concluded that a large portion (over 75%) of the workforce was not really motivated (engaged) and thus unable to achieve the goals of the organization. Only around one in four workers were focused on the company's goals; the rest were just showing up and collecting a paycheck. They did not actually say "that," but one could easily conclude that that was what was happening.

So, the question is, in a "knowledge economy" what is the best way to motivate yourself and others?

The answer is simple but, as they say, not easy.

The answer lies in answering the question *"What's in it for me?"* Think about the question. We do most of the things we do for the benefits they provide us and others. In this case or the case at work, we do things because we believe they will benefit us, in some way.

Effective leaders can communicate, with passion, *what is in it* for all. They can see, with clarity, what is in it for members of the team. What's more, they can communicate, "what's in it" to all. They help others see what they will get if the goal is achieved. They can help others see how they will benefit and that they will be better off if the goal is achieved.

Most of us want to be part of something bigger than ourselves. When we are considering motivation, how to be motivated and how to motivate others, we are stepping into what I call the "Twilight Zone," i.e., a place where few ever go and a destination to which even fewer ever arrive.

So, remember that motivation of yourself and others leans heavily on your ability to see and help others see that what needs to be done is a task that brings us all closer to the goal, i.e., being able to passionately communicate a meaningful benefit to ourselves and for others.

Chapter VI

Crediting

How Am I Doing?

Once, when I was younger, I had the fortune to lead a group toward a goal of excellence. The group was much better than I was, and, while we did well, we finished last among a couple of dozen other similar units in commercial insurance sales. I was not particularly disappointed about the results because, as I told myself, I really didn't care about that statistic (that happens a lot in the workplace). So, I sat, thinking about other things, while they gave appropriate credit to those who **did** believe the goal was important.

At the end of the presentation, the BIG DOG (regional manager) said, "I have one more award." He pulled out a big trophy and said, "Now to the manager and his team that made the greatest <u>improvement</u> in commercial production over the last year." My name was on the trophy, and, while somewhat embarrassed, I rose and, with pride I might say, accepted the award.

Now that story is likely not too unique, but what followed was. Never did our team finish last again; most often our team finished among the top two or three and often first. That story represents, clearly, what a little crediting (albeit creative crediting) can do and points to the fact that there is always something good in almost everything.

Pat Williams, an author, speaker, Sunday school teacher, father of 19 children (only four of which were his own; the rest were adopted), wrote a book with Jim Denney called *Leadership Excellence*. In it, he talks about leadership in the twenty-first century. They wrote a section on *Servant Leadership*, which said, "Leadership is a job, not a position," and, most importantly, they wrote, "The people with which you work are not **your** people, **you** are theirs." How profound is that? You give yourself away, not to just anyone but to the people with whom you work or the people with whom you guide.

Some of the most frequent and effective "creditors" were your mom and dad. I know you often put their comments in the "what you are supposed to do" column, but you know, as I think back, it was my mom and dad who frequently gave me praise that I, often, did not deserve. They praised me for Bs an Cs on a report card, they gave me credit for playing a ballgame, well, when I was lousy, and they pointed to my potential far more times than I could count. They were big "Creditors."

The cost of crediting is not high, so why not invest it and observe the results? It is true that humans want to know how they are doing, but, sometimes, giving credit and praise when they are not due can pay dividends. Consider the value of lifting others up despite their mistakes.

Chapter VII

Emotional Intelligence

Making the Difference

A larger vocabulary is good but developing your emotional intelligence is even better. Let's talk about emotional intelligence first because it applies to both talking and listening.

First, emotional intelligence is a learned skill. People get more emotional intelligence (EI) simply by getting older (usually). Here are the main parts of EI: **self-awareness**, **social awareness**, **self-management**, **social management**, and **motivation**. It has been said by several different sources that you cannot be a good leader without a higher level of EI. I believe that. So, let's look at the five simple components of EI.

Self-Awareness. Most people think they are self-aware, but they are not. As you might conclude, self-awareness is all about knowing yourself. Many of us only want to look upon the good and not the bad, so often large gaps in self-awareness appear. But obviously you can get better here. You can come to know yourself more intimately, and that is what self-awareness is all about.

Social Awareness is simply self-awareness extended to others. Being able to understand and have an impact on those outside ourselves is a skill. Some know themselves well but cannot extend that knowledge to others. Being able to understand the intent or the mentality of those outside ourselves is a critical piece to leadership.

Self-Management is simply being able to manage what you know about yourself and to add to the skill set you have already.

Social Management is about your ability to manage those outside yourself.

Motivation. What is your level of motivation?

Thus, emotional intelligence is to leadership what knowledge and experience are to job performance. If you are standing at the "elevator door," the button that opens the door is backed by your knowledge and experience. You can walk in, but the elevator goes nowhere. It is not until you punch the button on the inside that the elevator begins to move. Your level is determined by your emotional intelligence. The more EI you have, the higher you can go.

Now we can go on with the talking and the listening. My suggestion is to get yourself into a mode of listening most of the time, i.e., talk 20 percent and listen 80 percent of the time. Learn to become an active listener. Let others know you are listening through your "body language." Lean forward, look the person in the eye, shake your head yes or no, and have some questions ready. These are just a few things you can do to make someone else feel important.

When you talk, do so briefly and learn to ask questions that expand your knowledge and give the other time to fill in some of the blanks.

Chapter VIII

Amygdala Hijacking, Moods, and Other Things

Where and what is this thing called the amygdala? Possibly the best way to identify this interesting part of the brain and the part that often plays an important role in our behavior is to build the brain from outside in. In doing so, we can get a grasp of where the amygdala lies and get some idea about what it does.

To begin, the brain and its necessary parts are often referred to as the central nervous system or the brain, and the brain or cerebrum is divided into two hemispheres: the right and the left, which are joined together by the corpus callosum, a collection of nerve fibers that perform an important integrative role.

Each cerebral hemisphere is covered by what is called the "cerebral cortex" and includes several different lobes, e.g., occipital, parietal, temporal, and frontal. The insular cortex and the hippocampus, parts of the cerebral cortex, are not seen when observing the brain without dissection. Underneath all this are bunches of ganglia, one of which is the amygdala; the other two, the basal ganglia, and the basal forebrain form the diencephalon (a combination of the thalamus and hypothalamus). All of this and a few other items are connected to every part of our bodies by nerves that are sometimes called brain cells and are composed of both neurons and axons. Thus, the connection of the central nervous system with the body is handled by nerves.

It was possibly Dan Goleman, an early advocate of emotional intelligence, who first coined the phrase "amygdala hijacking." The amygdala is part of the interior brain that is focused on recognizing fear and sending the message to the body from danger. It receives input from the senses and processes them ever so quickly and sends what it knows to the pre-frontal cortex, i.e., the organization center of the brain. Sometimes the amygdala and or the prefrontal cortex make mistakes. Sometimes the amygdala, when it is hijacked by outside stimulus sends a danger signal that is, well, let's say "overstated," like mistaking a garden hose for a snake. Anyway, amygdala hijacking refers to those times when the amygdala, doing its job, sends a danger message that causes the prefrontal cortex to decide what to do in an inappropriate manner. When that happens, it is called "amygdala hijacking."

Now moods are consistently making their presence known. But first, just what are moods? I think the best explanation is that moods are emotions that are dissipated and lengthened. Moods are initiated by emotion and last much longer. Moods come in two general categories: GOOD and BAD. Moods influence the intensity of emotion, i.e., a good mood extends the emotion of joy or a bad mood makes it easier to anger. So, you can see that, depending upon the type of mood (good or bad), one might experience emotional swings that are disproportionate with the situation.

Possibly the over-riding thought here is that both moods and emotion influence the thought process. Moods and emotion influence the way we think, e.g., the emotion of anxiety can reduce the working memory capacity and problem-solving capability by distracting us from the task at hand. Moods can influence the way people make judgments and predictions. The emotion of fear, for instance, tends to pull us toward pessimistic judgments of the future. Individuals in a good mood, on the other hand, tend to remember more and better. Overall, moods and emotion affect the way we think. Being aware of the moods we are in brings us one step closer to superior leadership, i.e., the goal.

Chapter XI

Leadership Lessons Learned

Changing the World

In his book, *Organizing Genius*, Warren Bennis with Patricia Biederman wrote that "Great groups tend to be islands of excellence that exist apart from their surroundings." No doubt, most leaders would settle for that, but the question is what makes that happen? He went on to share that great groups start with superior people who have original minds and want to do the next thing. Finding superior people begins with defining the word "superior." It is not likely that you or anyone else can ever find the place superior without first defining it.

Doing exceptional work would likely be a goal of both a good leader and the team he or she leads. So, looking back to the gathering of exceptional people, one might conclude that the group may go nowhere unless there are good people on board. Selecting superior performers for your group may be one of the most important things you will ever do.

In almost every instance, high-performing teams led by exceptional leaders are the foundation for exceptional results.

But exceptional people are not all that is required. There are many instances where great people and exceptional leaders have failed. The skill of organizing the energy and capability of the group is not one held by all. Great leaders are those individuals who can get the energy and intelligence of the group pointed toward the goal pursued and extract the energy from the group to move toward the achievement of the goal. Being able to apply the energy and talent of an exceptional group to the achievement of a goal is easier said than done. Teams filled with talented people can be an experience like "herding cats" or like skating on ice (things seem to have an energy of their own).

Bennis talks about teams taking on an almost perpetual image, one of never stopping. It is difficult to outperform a group that has all the answers and works all the time. That, I think, is an image of a superior led group. Smart and hard working. So, just to simplify, putting together "high-performing teams begins with gathering good people, influencing them and getting them focused on a worthwhile objective, moving them forward toward achieving that objective, encouraging them as you move toward the goal and finally but certainly not least, congratulating them on the progress made.

In all, leadership is a simple but not easy endeavor. It begins with an inspirational vision, moves through communication of that vision, in such a way that attracts followers. Then there must be a reasonable plan for the achievement of the objective and time to help ourselves and others to stay focused and be flexible while always moving toward the vision. Finally, there must be time for celebration when the goal is reached.

ALWAYS MOVING IN A POSITIVE DIRECTION!

References

Sylvia Ann Hewlett	*Executive Presence*	HarperCollins Business	2014
Daniel Pink	*Drive*	Riverhead Books	2009
Kravitz &Schubert	*Emotional Intelligence Works*	Crisp Publications	2000
Stein & Book	*The EQ Edge*	Jossey-Bass	2006
Adele Lynn	*The EQ Interview*	Amacom	2008
Daniel Goleman	*Emotional Intelligence*	Bantam	1995
Dylan Evans	*Emotion*	Oxford University Press	2001
Watts Wacker	*The Visionary's Handbook*	HarperCollins Publishing	2000
Su & Wilkens	*Own the Room*	Harvard Business Review	2013
Williams & Denney	*Leadership Excellence*	Barbour Publishing	2012
Antonio Damasio	*Self Comes to Mind*	Pantheon Books	2010
Daniel Goleman	*Social Intelligence*	Bantam	2006
Barbara Kellerman	*The End of Leadership*	HarperCollins Business	2012
Barbara Kellerman	*Leadership*	McGraw-Hill	2010
Barbara Kellerman	*Followership*	Harvard Business Press	2008
Bennis & Biederman	*Organizing Genius*	Basic Books	1997